Pastorale

by Deborah Eisenberg

| A Samuel French Acting Edition |

New York Hollywood London Toronto
SAMUELFRENCH.COM

Copyright © 1981, 1982 by Deborah Eisenberg

ALL RIGHTS RESERVED

CAUTION: Professionals and amateurs are hereby warned that *PASTORALE* is subject to a Licensing Fee. It is fully protected under the copyright laws of the United States of America, the British Commonwealth, including Canada, and all other countries of the Copyright Union. All rights, including professional, amateur, motion picture, recitation, lecturing, public reading, radio broadcasting, television and the rights of translation into foreign languages are strictly reserved. In its present form the play is dedicated to the reading public only.

The amateur live stage performance rights to *PASTORALE* are controlled exclusively by Samuel French, Inc., and licensing arrangements and performance licenses must be secured well in advance of presentation. PLEASE NOTE that amateur Licensing Fees are set upon application in accordance with your producing circumstances. When applying for a licensing quotation and a performance license please give us the number of performances intended, dates of production, your seating capacity and admission fee. Licensing Fees are payable one week before the opening performance of the play to Samuel French, Inc., at 45 W. 25th Street, New York, NY 10010.

Licensing Fee of the required amount must be paid whether the play is presented for charity or gain and whether or not admission is charged.

Stock licensing fees quoted upon application to Samuel French, Inc.

For all other rights than those stipulated above, apply to: Ellen Neuwald, Inc., 905 West End Ave., New York, NY 10025.

Particular emphasis is laid on the question of amateur or professional readings, permission and terms for which must be secured in writing from Samuel French, Inc.

Copying from this book in whole or in part is strictly forbidden by law, and the right of performance is not transferable.

Whenever the play is produced the following notice must appear on all programs, printing and advertising for the play: "Produced by special arrangement with Samuel French, Inc."

Due authorship credit must be given on all programs, printing and advertising for the play.

No one shall commit or authorize any act or omission by which the copyright of, or the right to copyright, this play may be impaired.
No one shall make any changes in this play for the purpose of production.
Publication of this play does not imply availability for performance. Both amateurs and professionals considering a production are strongly advised in their own interests to apply to Samuel French, Inc., for written permission before starting rehearsals, advertising, or booking a theatre.
No part of this book may be reproduced, stored in a retrieval system, or transmitted in any form, by any means, now known or yet to be invented, including mechanical, electronic, photocopying, recording, videotaping, or otherwise, without the prior written permission of the publisher.

ISBN 978-0-573-61363-0   Printed in U.S.A.   #18016

PASTORALE was first presented in New York City in April, 1982, at the Second Stage, whose Artistic Directors are Robyn Goodman and Carole Rothman. It was directed by Carole Rothman, the set design was by Heidi Landesman, the lighting by Frances Aronson, costumes by Nan Cibula, and the sound design by Gary Harris. The Production Stage Manager was James McConnell-Clark, Jr., the Stage Manager was Rebecca Pease, Kim Novick was the Production Supervisor for the Second Stage, and Drew Farber the Associate Director. Casting was by Meg Simon and Fran Kumin. The cast, in order of appearance, was as follows:

MELANIE .... Judith Ivey

RACHEL .... Christine Estabrook

STEVE .... Thomas Waites

MAN .... Howard Renensland

EDIE .... Elizabeth Austin

JOHN .... Jeffrey Fahey

CELIA .... Taylor Miller

COLORADANS .... David B. Hunt, Bjorn Johnson, Paul Loughlin

WOMAN .... Rebecca Pease

CAST

Men
   Steve
   Man
   John
   and, if possible, 3 guys from Colorado

Women
   Melanie
   Rachel
   Edie
   Celia

There should also be a Couple, who appear very briefly. If necessary, however, the Couple could be played as a Woman (by a woman) or as a Man (by a man.)

MELANIE

RACHEL

STEVE

EDIE *and*

JOHN *are in their mid-20's. It may seem to you that they are younger, but they are not.*

the MAN *is around 28 or 30*

CELIA *is 19 or 20*

the COUPLE *who arrive at the end of February should be in their late 20's or early 30's. They are self-possessed and relaxed. They are chic and dressed in jeans or corderoys, maybe, and Frye boots.*

The play until the end of the final scene takes place entirely in the central room of a farmhouse. A door leading to Melanie's room is visible. Also opening directly onto this room, either visibly or not, are doors leading to the outside and to the kitchen. Somewhere in this house is a room in which Rachel stays. Perhaps it is directly off this room, or perhaps it isn't.

JUNE

MELANIE. So why don't you just drop it? I mean, what do you care?
RACHEL. It's true. I know. I don't even know the guy, but I've got this horrible crush on him anyhow.
STEVE. How did you guys get together?
RACHEL. Well, I met him one day a month or two ago. He was passing through the city on his way to Europe and he didn't know anybody, so I said he could come over and stay for a couple of nights. So anyhow, he just kind of eventually was still there. Sometimes I'd come home from work and he'd have made cookies or something, and sometimes he said these really terrific things. And I got to really like sleeping with him. I mean, I didn't ever get to know him that well, but—
STEVE. And then he left for Europe, huh?
RACHEL. Well, not exactly. What it is, is when I was laid off I went to Colorado for a couple of weeks until my unemployment started, and I left him in the apartment, and when I got back it turned out he had moved in with my sort-of friend Pammy on 6th Street.
STEVE. It's too bad you feel so bad about him.
RACHEL. Well, yes, but really I don't. At least I don't actually care about him, really. That's a whole other thing, thank God. I mean, I know I won't feel

like this too long, and besides, it's not a very important sort of feeling. And also, it's not, you know, very closely related to the person I feel it about.

STEVE. Well, but Rachel—I mean, that's always all that's going on. I mean, you just have some sort of feeling, you know, scanning your field, and somebody wanders into its trajectory, is all.

RACHEL. Could be. Well, but what if, say, you're actually in love with someone, though. Well, maybe not love . . . but, oh—friends. You only feel friendship about people who are actually your friends.

STEVE. Well, but friendship isn't exactly a feeling, though, in that sense.

RACHEL. Oh, yeah. True. You know, I'm really glad I came up this weekend. We all should keep in touch more.

MELANIE. Why don't you just stay up here for the summer?

STEVE. Yeah, why go back to all that pavement. Summer in the city. God. The city's so overloaded anyway.

RACHEL. It's true there's a lot of jumping around for I don't know what. I'm always so wired, but I can't think what I've really been doing. Sometimes I wish I could just, you know, stop.

STEVE. God. I wish I could just start.

MELANIE. You know, there's plenty of room here, if you want to stay.

RACHEL. It would be great, but I've really got to go back and get a job.

MELANIE. You could get a job up here, though. Matter of fact, I'm going to talk to some lady at the

pottery place this afternoon about a job, and I'll ask for you, too. This house is really a good deal, besides. It's practically free. Remember Ruthie Fisher? She got it for me. The owners have moved to Connecticut, and they want someone in the house till it gets sold. All I have to do is see if any kids fall in the well and take out the dead mice my cats bring in and stuff.
  MAN. (*From off*) Hey, Melanie!
  MELANIE. Oh. GOODMORNING! Shit.
  RACHEL. What's that?
  MELANIE. Some guy I managed to pry loose from the bar at the Ironstone. Too bad you were asleep when I got in. You missed an enchanting little entertainment. Me absolutely desperate to haul him into bed, and him absolutely glued to the sofa, telling me that a young woman like me should watch out for the venal characters that hang around the bars in town. Actually he was so ripped he couldn't stand up. Furthermore, he was so boring I almost just had to toss him out on his ass. Basically, though, I'm a very patient person.
  RACHEL. Gosh. Well, at least your patience was rewarded.
  MELANIE. Not particularly well. Wish I could remember his name, though. Horrible breach of etiquette, huh?
  MAN. Melanie! Got any aspirin?
  MELANIE. Coming right away, there, uh... Lamb Chop. (MELANIE *goes to her room.*)
  STEVE. Why not stick around, Rache? We could all have a lot of fun.

RACHEL. Wish I could.

(MELANIE *returns*)

MELANIE. Anybody need anything from the store?
RACHEL. Cookies!
MELANIE. O.K. (MELANIE *exits*)
RACHEL. It's nice to see Melanie again.
STEVE. She's changed a lot since school, you know. People around here are sort of concerned about her, in fact.
RACHEL. Really? Why?
STEVE. Well, those people in town disapprove of her, essentially, and everyone we know around here considers her, you know, extreme. And she is quite, well, observable, a lot of the time.
RACHEL. She never was a hypocrite.
STEVE. Well, she's a bit farther along the line than non-hypocrisy these days. I mean, she's fine, but it's not what people want, exactly. And she does lie, occasionally, too, which isn't ideal.
RACHEL. She does?
STEVE. Well, not about anything big. But things like, one day we were over at Edie's and someone asked Melanie where she got her ring, and she said she got it in Tashkent. But actually, I happen to know she got it in Townsend, cause I was with her at the time. Just stuff like that. Little things.
RACHEL. God. That's too bad. But in a way it doesn't matter, I don't think. Because, I mean, if someone says something, it's true, isn't it? I mean, it's true because either they intend it, or they want it to be that way, or they believe it is that way ...

STEVE. That's what I used to think, but now I think—
MAN. (*Emerging*) Morning.
RACHEL. Oh. Gosh!
STEVE. Hey.
MAN. Where's Melanie?
RACHEL. I don't know, really. She left.
STEVE. She had to do something.
MAN. Oh. You her roommates?
RACHEL. Oh, we don't have roommates. Oh, actually, Steve does. Steve lives over in the valley with some friends of ours.
MAN. Well, that's nice, Steve. And what about you —do you live anywhere?
RACHEL. Oh, yes!
MAN. Now that's what I call a coincidence.
RACHEL. Oh. I see. No, I live in the city.
MAN. Must be fun. Like it there?
RACHEL. Well, I'm not sure. I mean, I'm not there right now, so I can't tell. I mean right now I'm here, and I like it, even though of course I can't tell exactly, because I don't have anything to compare it to. I mean, you can't really know how how you feel about a place, unless you can be in some other place at the same time.
MAN. Is she . . . ?
STEVE. Huh?
MAN. Any coffee around here?
STEVE. Yeah. Some in there.
MAN. Anybody else want some?
STEVE. Yeah, thanks.
RACHEL. Oh, me too!
MAN. How about half a cup, in case you're having

one somewhere else now, too?

STEVE. Rachel just likes to get things straight, is all.

RACHEL. That's true! That's right! Oh, Steve. That's what was so disconcerting about this business with Paul. See, I had thought our relationship grew out of his wanting a place to stay, but actually it grew out of his wanting someone to stay with. So everything I had thought was going on all during it was really just completely grounded in error!

STEVE. Well, you know, Rache, you can't decide all by yourself what's going on with you and other people, because it happens in the middle of you, you know? And besides, it keeps changing while it's going on.

RACHEL. True. Well, what do you mean, though?

STEVE. Well, I mean, you don't look out the window and see the woods and say, "Oh, that tree looks so nice and so does that one. And so does that one over there." I mean, you don't go out in the rain and think, "Well, the first 17 drops made me damp, and the next 42 will get me wet, and 31 more will keep me wet, and the 60th will get me really drenched." You know?

MAN. You're not going to believe this, but I was just about to make that very point myself.

STEVE. Huh? Oh, was there any cream left in there, by the way?

RACHEL. Oh, I see what you mean, I think. I mean, I think...

AUGUST

RACHEL. I think your new girlfriend is terrific, Steve.

STEVE. She really is, isn't she? I'm really in love. She's so smart, you know, and pretty. She's so, sort of, sweet and clean, like a little toy train, or something. I'm so crazy about her. I really just want to spirit her away into the forest and live in the branches and sing and eat fruit and drink wine out of silver goblets our relatives send us—

RACHEL. Are you going to get a place together?

STEVE. Well, no, actually. She'll have to go back to her dorm in the fall, and her parents would hit the roof anyhow. And besides, I feel like I'd really like to live alone for a while. It's been pretty rough over at Sue and Edie's recently.

RACHEL. How come?

STEVE. Well, too many people cruising through, for one thing. And Fred is really getting to me. I mean, at first I really enjoyed him, but the novelty is definitely wearing off.

MELANIE. I can see why. He is revolting, after all.

STEVE. Oh, I don't mind that. But he teaches some sort of, like, political philosophy to little kids at that experimental school in Leamingham, and he sort of forgets to stop when he comes home. Between him and Sue there's a system for everything at that house. There are grocery-shopping systems, and dinner-cooking systems, and floor-sweeping systems, and plant-watering systems. And Edie's pretty automated herself. They're even sort of regimented about their dope. And Sue and Keith are always enacting these tragic endings to their epic love. It's just so Teutonic over there. Besides, Sue says I'm a slob.

RACHEL. Oh, slobs. God. I'm such a slob. How can you stand it, Melanie? You're so neat. How can you live with a slob like me?

MELANIE. Well, I don't really mind. I've been thinking about it, in fact, and it's occured to me that it's probably harder to learn to be neat than to learn to be a slob, so I thought maybe I'd try to be a slob, too, so we don't get, you know, tense about the whole thing. I bet I could get into it. I mean, actually, I'm really tired of taking out those disgusting dead mice my cats bring in, for instance. I think I'm just going to put coffee cups over them. And I'm definitely too compulsive about the dishes. I'm going to try to leave them in the sink for a while from now on.

RACHEL. Oh, hey, speaking of dirty dishes, is there anything to eat around here?

MELANIE. Well, there's some left over meat loaf.

RACHEL. The loaded meat loaf? No thanks. Any chocolate?

MELANIE. All out. I could make some eggs.

RACHEL. Phooey.

MELANIE. How about a shot of bourbon?

RACHEL. What I really want is some cookies or something.

MELANIE. Well, I guess I'll just have to drink that bourbon myself.

STEVE. Anybody want to go for a swim?

RACHEL. You know, it occurs to me I've really got to get a job just about instantly. I'm really almost totally out of money.

STEVE. Well, I'm doing all right with this construction job. I could carry you for a while.

RACHEL. Oh, thanks, Steve, but I really can't do that. Besides, I've been coasting a bit on Melanie, and she's almost broke.

PASTORALE

MELANIE. The thing is to not get hysterical about it. The pottery thing almost worked out, after all. Besides, we know a lot of people around here who could get us something.

STEVE. It's true. I know everybody at all the bars in Townsend and Whitfield. Tomorrow, I absolutely promise, I'll take you two around and we'll get you both jobs.

MELANIE. Oh, rapture.

STEVE. So listen, are we going swimming or not?

MELANIE. It's getting kind of late.

RACHEL. I don't think I can really handle getting all undressed and then having to get dressed again. I feel like I've done it so often recently.

MELANIE. Why don't you call Celia, Steve? She could come over or something.

STEVE. Well, I don't know. Her sister just had a baby, so she's really busy for a while.

RACHEL. Well.

MELANIE. We could go to the movies.

STEVE. If there was anything in town we wanted to see, which there isn't.

RACHEL. We could go visit Edie and Sue.

STEVE. I just left them. Want to go into Townsend for a drink?

RACHEL. Too early.

MELANIE. Arts and crafts? Fun and games? Show and tell?

STEVE. Live and learn?

MELANIE. Well, ok, but like, anything in particular? I mean, what do we want to do?

STEVE. This, I guess. I mean, this is what we're doing.

SEPTEMBER

(STEVE *and* RACHEL *are asleep on the floor or sofas*)

STEVE. Oh, that sun! Christ!
RACHEL. Umf.
STEVE. Glad I fell asleep here. I never would have made it home.
RACHEL. Specially since you left your car at The Distant Drum.
STEVE. Did I? Oh, right. Melanie drove back, didn't she. Jesus. That was awful. Aren't you afraid to drive around with her?
RACHEL. A little. Usually she isn't that bad, though.
STEVE. She couldn't be. Think these are aspirin?
RACHEL. They look a little small.
STEVE. I'd sure like them to be aspirin.
RACHEL. Well, ok.
EDIE. (*Appearing*) Hi. I was just on my way to the Grand Union and thought I'd drop by to see how you were. Hi, Steve. How's your new place?
STEVE. Oh, great. How's the house? How's Sue doing? I hear Fred moved out.
EDIE. Yeah. He and Sue had a big fight about the dinner-cooking system. On the weeks he was in charge all he ever bought was chicken. And Count Chocula. Every night during his weeks we ate broiled chicken. Which was better than it could have been. I mean, who doesn't like broiled chicken? Except us, now. We hate it. Besides, it was really unfair. He was the one who set up the system, and the rest of us would

really, you know, try to make these actual meals, which was at the very least a fantastic pain in the ass, and all he did was just make 45 pounds of broiled chicken every Monday. That's all we ever got to eat, plus Count Chocula.

RACHEL. I like Count Chocula.

EDIE. Yeah, it's good. But we never even had any milk to go with it!

STEVE. So is anybody else living there now?

EDIE. Well, there's this sort of religious couple, Mark and Louise. I don't know exactly what their religion is, but it's very quiet. Unfortunately, they're also real pigs. And Sanford's there until he finishes the place he's building.

RACHEL. Sounds good.

EDIE. So it's too bad about you and Melanie getting fired.

RACHEL. Wow. News travels fast.

EDIE. It didn't have far to go. I was standing right next to you.

RACHEL. You know, there may be some stuff I can't remember too clearly about last night.

EDIE. So are you pissed off at Melanie?

RACHEL. No. Why?

EDIE. Well, I mean, she got you fired, really, didn't she.

RACHEL. Oh, I don't know. They're so stuffy at that place. As if they were running a real restaurant, you know? I mean it's basically just a bar, when you get right down to it, and a pretty elemental one at that. And to take on about Melanie like that! It was so pointless.

EDIE. Well, I mean, she does act like a maniac, after all. And she probably drinks half their profit.

RACHEL. Well, they could have thought of that a while ago. Alain was just irritated cause she was acting like that while his wife was around.

EDIE. I still don't understand why they fired you too.

RACHEL. Oh, I don't know. I suppose they had to. I mean, I haven't slept with any of them, and Melanie's slept with all of them. So they couldn't have just fired her without feeling pretty foolish. And besides, I really am a terrible waitress—anything I don't forget, I drop.

EDIE. You know, if you want to move in with us you can.

RACHEL. Thanks. Really.

EDIE. I mean, I think life's probably a lot simpler over at our place.

(MELANIE *enters*)

STEVE. How's Sue doing with Keith these days? Is that going any better?

EDIE. Well, I don't think so. He keeps telling her he cares about her, and then he'll show up somewhere with some girl, or he won't call her, or he'll just get all weird and remote all of a sudden. And she spends all of her time trying to, you know, get all the information into some digestible form. I mean, she sits around thinking, 'Oh, I made him feel this, so he's doing that,' or, 'Oh, I wonder what this means that he's acting like that,' when the truth is nothing he does means anything. He's just an asshole.

MELANIE. Whenever I see them together, it doesn't really look like he's very interested in her.
EDIE. Well, he is, in his nasty little way.
MELANIE. He's always coming on to other women.
EDIE. No he isn't. He just likes to have a big effect on everyone.
MELANIE. Well, he seems pretty serious. I mean about coming on to other women.
EDIE. It's just bullshit. It wouldn't fool a child.
STEVE. Melanie, are these aspirin?
MELANIE. Jesus. No.
STEVE. What would they do to me if I took them?
MELANIE. The question is what would I do to you if you took them. Does everybody want coffee? I'll go make some. (*She exits*)
EDIE. Boy. Melanie's sure gotten a lot worse.
RACHEL. Wow. (*Long silence*) Worse than what?
EDIE. Worse than she used to be.
RACHEL. Well, he really does come on to her. I've seen him.
EDIE. Well, but he can't stand her. He says so.
MELANIE. (*Entering*) Who wants breakfast?
STEVE. I want aspirin.
RACHEL. Breakfast? Oh, boy. Can we have french toast?
MELANIE. Sure. Going to stick around, Edie?
EDIE. No. I have to get to work. Thanks, though.
MELANIE. Are you still working for Jeremy whatsisname?
EDIE. Yeah. I'm doing my textiles for him now. He's selling them in lengths, and they're actually doing pretty well.

MELANIE. Yes? That's fabulous. You know what—you should have me and Rachel make some up into dresses for the store. We could probably make some money that way, and it would be really good for you.

RACHEL. I can't sew.

EDIE. Well, maybe. I don't know.

MELANIE. Why don't you talk to Jeremy about it?

EDIE. Well, can you do stuff in true sizes and stuff, and could you hand finish them?

MELANIE. Why not?

EDIE. Well, I don't know. I'll talk to Jeremy maybe. But we've just started this deal, and I don't want to screw it up.

MELANIE. Why would that screw it up?

EDIE. Oh, I don't know. Ok, I'll talk to him sometime.

STEVE. Does anybody have any aspirin?

MELANIE. Sure, help yourself. In my night table drawer.

EDIE. Well, ok. I've gotta go. Steve, why don't you bring your girlfriend over sometime. We really want to meet her.

STEVE. Sure. (*He wanders out to get aspirin*)

EDIE. Oh, and Rachel—Sue really wants to see you. You should stop by.

RACHEL. Great.

EDIE. See you guys soon.

STEVE. (*Crossing to kitchen*) Bye.

(EDIE *exits*)

MELANIE. Want bacon with your french toast?

PASTORALE 21

RACHEL. Sure! Great!

(MELANIE *exits*)

STEVE. (*Returning with aspirin and water*) Ah. Relief.
RACHEL. Work fast, huh?
STEVE. Actually, they don't work at all, I don't think. But I take them anyhow. I mean, you have to take the plunge, right? It may look like a sequence of empty gestures, but it just might turn out to be real life.
RACHEL. Hey, Steve? How come Edie's so weird with Melanie? I mean she really seems to hate Melanie.
STEVE. Yeah, that's true. I don't really know why. I mean, Melanie is... well, I don't know... I mean I know Edie thinks it's really ridiculous that Melanie wears false eyelashes, and... well, she thinks Melanie's a terrible driver, but so do I—I mean, I don't really know.
RACHEL. Oh! I forgot to tell you. Melanie and I ran into Celia yesterday.
STEVE. Where?
RACHEL. In town.
STEVE. Where in town? What was she doing? Was she with anyone? What did she say?
RACHEL. We saw her in Harold's. She was very sweet. We just talked for a minute. You should bring her by sometime.
STEVE. I'd really like to. I'd really like to. What was she doing in Harold's do you think?
RACHEL. She was buying a notebook or something.

I don't know. Steve?

STEVE. Huh? Where did I put that glass of water. Oh, man. Ah, there. What?

RACHEL. Nothin'.

MELANIE. (*Enters*) Coffee?

RACHEL AND STEVE. Wow, great. Fantastic.

RACHEL. Maybe this afternoon we should look for a new job or something.

MELANIE. Oh, God. This afternoon. Listen, the season will be starting soon. We aren't going to have any trouble.

RACHEL. Well, I haven't saved anything up. And I want to be able to go back to New York with something.

MELANIE. Well, besides. We can probably work something out with Edie and Jeremy. Listen. We had a very rough night last night, we really did. And I think it's important just not to worry about anything today. We should really try not to worry.

NOVEMBER

MELANIE. Oh, God. You know what? I'm supposed to have those samples for Edie Friday morning.

STEVE. Do you have a lot left to do?

MELANIE. Well, basically, yes. I mean, I haven't really started.

STEVE. Wow. Well, maybe John and I should leave so you could do them.

MELANIE. I don't think that would help really.

STEVE. Anything I could do?
MELANIE. Can you sew?
STEVE. Uh uh.
MELANIE. Neither can I, as it turns out. I thought I could when I told Edie I'd do the dresses. I don't really know why it didn't occur to me I couldn't. You know how that happens sometimes?
STEVE. Sort of. I'm not sure. What about Rachel?
MELANIE. Oh you know Rachel. She just says, "I can't sew, I can't sew."
STEVE. Can Rachel sew?
MELANIE. Rachel? Of course not.
STEVE. Where is Rachel anyway?
MELANIE. She's working tonight over at the Wellspring. She should be back any time now. Marty Patera's dropping her off on his way home.
JOHN. (*Who has been reading catalogues or comic books*) Who's Rachel?
MELANIE. She lives here.
JOHN. Yeah?
STEVE. So should we do something about those dresses?
MELANIE. Well. The first thing we should do is have a drink. Then, if nothing occurs to us by tomorrow, I'll just call Edie and explain.
STEVE. Well at least nobody's depending on them or anything.
MELANIE. Nope. I mean, a couple of people have ordered them, but, you know.
STEVE. Oops. Oh, well.
MELANIE. Yeah. Good thing Jeremy gave me an advance.

STEVE. Jesus. How did you ever get that miser to give you an advance?
MELANIE. Oh, I went for a drink with him, and I was very, uh, charming. And I told him I couldn't possibly do anything without an advance. Which was true. I bought that sewing machine with the advance.
STEVE. Useful investment, huh.
MELANIE. And some other stuff besides, of course. It only cost 20 bucks. So who wants something to drink?
JOHN. Me. What is there?
MELANIE. Gin. Tonic, anyone? Some lemon? (*She is peeling a lemon toward herself*) You know, whenever I do this, I always picture the blade in my heart.

(RACHEL *enters*)

STEVE. The one of those I do most is when someone bumps into me, sometimes, I'm so enraged I see myself just grabbing them and hurling them into the wall, or turning around and pushing them off the bus as hard as I can.
MELANIE. Yeah, that one. Another thing I always see is me on the windshield of some car, or flying through my own windshield. It's so slow and vivid. I can feel each of my bones impacting with the glass, and then the glass gives and shatters, and I see it glittering and I feel my blood bursting out—
RACHEL. You know what really scares me? I'm always afraid I'm going to grab food off the plate of the person sitting next to me in a restaurant. You know, when you come in and sit down, and you're hungry, and the people next to you are just sitting

there talking, and there's this food on their plates, and sometimes it just sort of starts singing to you?
JOHN. Singing to you. Oh shit.
MELANIE. Hi, Rache. Want some gin?
RACHEL. Yes. No. Maybe I better not. I just took some acid, I think
MELANIE. Well, do you think you did? Or do you think you know you did? Or what?
RACHEL. Oh, well, I guess I know I did.
STEVE. I didn't think you did that stuff.
RACHEL. I didn't. But I just did. So I guess now I do. I mean, I suppose I wouldn't have, but Marty and I stopped for gas in Leamingham and he took a tab, and he handed one to me and he said, "Here. Take this," so I did.

(*Horrible silence*)

RACHEL. Was that a bad thing to do?
MELANIE. Oh, no! It's fine!
STEVE. Fine!
RACHEL. What do you mean! Oh, no, oh God. I'm going to go insane, aren't I! I'm going to be insane the entire rest of my life!
STEVE. No, uh uh. You'll be fine! It'll be fun. We'll be right here, and you'll have a lot of fun!
RACHEL. Oh, God. Oh, God.

(*Long silence during which* JOHN *gets up and gets a piece of fruit, which he eats slowly and noisily.*)

RACHEL. You know, another thing that I'm always afraid of is that I'm going to touch people.

JOHN. Like, what do you mean?

RACHEL. Well, I mean, sometimes don't you ever think when someone's sitting right near you that you could just so easily? You know, reach over and stroke their leg or something? I mean, sometimes I'll be standing in line behind somebody, or something, and I really want to put my hand on their face or kiss their neck or something. I mean I'm just suddenly so aware of this person's body being right there. And I just sometimes really feel like touching this person's body.

MELANIE. More gin?

JOHN. Sure. (*As* MELANIE *pours gin in his glass, he runs his hand up her leg. They remain thus affiliated for the first part of his speech*) I remember once I was at this concert, and there was this chick sitting in the seat next to me. And she was, like, older, but she was pretty good looking, and she looked really, really sad. Well, I remember I had just washed my hair, which was pretty long then, and it was all sort of electric. And I realized it was sort of brushing against this woman when I'd turn around, and I wondered if it was annoying her. But then I noticed she was beginning to lean a bit towards me when I'd turn, and also I saw that she was sort of looking at my hands. I mean, I really wasn't sure, so I rolled up my sleeves, really slowly. Like this... And I sort of stretched my arms out on the arm rests. Well she was definitely looking at my arms. No question about it. So, I was staring at the stage like I was really absorbed in the concert, and I leaned my head just a little bit towards her. Well, first she put her arm sort of over the back

of my seat, like she was just sitting there, but pretty
soon her hand started, just really, really gently playing with my hair, and I pretended not to notice, but I
sort of moved my head around a bit. (*He reaches out
and pulls the transfixed* MELANIE *onto his lap*) That's
right, honey. Climb on aboard. So anyway, after a bit
she was really getting into it, you know? And so I
just, like I didn't notice what I was doing, put my
hand down, right so the back of my hand was just
touching her leg, and then I moved it. Just a bit, but
noticably. Well, she practically just melted over into
my seat with me, and she was crying like crazy, but
completely silent. Oh, God, it was so weird—her
tears were sort of pouring around my neck, and she
was unbuttoning my shirt, and running her hand, like
inside the top of my jeans, just sobbing away, but
completely quiet. Christ, was that freaky.

(*Long silence.* JOHN *and* MELANIE *neck in the chair
with great intensity.* STEVE *and* RACHEL *sit*)

STEVE. Think that means I'm going to shove some-
one off a bus?
MELANIE. So what happened then?
JOHN. When?
MELANIE. Well, I mean, at the end of the concert.
JOHN. Well, it was the end of the concert. I left.
MELANIE. With the woman?
JOHN. Nah. She was with some other chick any-
way.
RACHEL. I think that might be very ...
STEVE. Don't focus on it.

(JOHN *and* MELANIE *are again absorbed in necking*)

RACHEL. You know what, Steve?
STEVE. What.
RACHEL. You're not going to shove anyone off a bus!
STEVE. Oh, probably not. Anyhow, it's nothing to worry about.
RACHEL. No, but it is! I'm really serious, because it's really important! I mean I never really knew this was true until right now, but it is—this thing is true— THERE ARE DIFFERENT SORTS OF PEOPLE!
JOHN. What a piece of work.
MELANIE. She's my friend.
RACHEL. I mean you always wonder, well, are people all the same, and they just get screwed up in various different ways, but basically everyone's the same, and everyone *could* shove someone off the bus or toss someone out the window or chop some guy's arm off at the shoulder, but only some people *do*, and that's just completely because of circumstances, like there's a war or someone in the same room makes them so angry they just have to, which could happen to anybody.
MELANIE. Let's go into my room.
JOHN. I sort of like it here.
RACHEL. But that's not right! See, the real reason that some people do and some people don't is that people differ from one another! I mean at least in this way, which has got to be, like, chemical, probably. Because when you think about it, it's like what kind of food you like. I mean, I really like, uh, let's see... banana

bread! You know? But some people just don't. And it's probably true that they really basically don't, because there isn't that much that can deeply influence you with food. I mean, there are some things, obviously, that can, like if your mother mashes olives into your hair when she gets mad at you when you're a kid, you probably won't like olives, but it's probably going to be restricted to pretty narrow particulars, like you might not like olives, but you probably won't not like all oval foods, even though on the same basis you might sort of learn to not like all people. What was I talking about? Wait—

JOHN. Ok. You want to go to your room?

MELANIE. Wait a sec.

JOHN. Are you going to have to do something about her?

MELANIE. No. What do you mean? (JOHN *exits to* MELANIE's *room*) Hey, Rache.

RACHEL. Hi, Melanie.

MELANIE. Hi. Listen, Rachel. There are two things I have to say, and I want you to remember them. Ok?

RACHEL. Ok. Yes.

MELANIE. See these? These are my false eyelashes. A little later it may occur to you that they're wiggling. But they won't be. So don't squash them, please, ok?

RACHEL. Ok. How many things was that?

MELANIE. Huh? Oh. One thing.

RACHEL. How can you tell?

MELANIE. Well... cause, I mean, cause I know. I mean, I know it's one thing cause it's all in the same, uh... category.

RACHEL. It is? Well, how come everything isn't in that category.

MELANIE. No. What I mean is, it's one thing because I mean, I'm the person who's talking, so I get to decide how many things it is. No, wait, I mean... oh, shit. Trust me.

RACHEL. I do trust you, Melanie. I really, really trust you.

JOHN. Hey.

MELANIE. Coming. Good night, Rache.

RACHEL. Good night. You be ok?

MELANIE. Sure. Of course. Oh! The other thing is...

RACHEL. Don't make this one too hard...

MELANIE. ...is, if you want to, remember you can wake me up.

RACHEL. I can!? Really!?

MELANIE. Yeah, like if Steve goes home and you get...

RACHEL. Get..

MELANIE. No, it's ok. I mean, if you just happen to feel like company, just wake me up. I won't mind.

JOHN. Hey!

MELANIE. Coming.

RACHEL. Melanie?

MELANIE. Yeah, Rache?

RACHEL. Goodnight, Melanie.

MELANIE. Goodnight, Rachel.

STEVE. Goodnight, Melanie.

MELANIE. Goodnight, Steve.

JOHN. For Chrissake.

PASTORALE 31

MELANIE. Here I am.

(*They exit*)

STEVE. Well, I guess that concludes the video portion of tonight's broadcast.
RACHEL. No it doesn't. There's this sort of wallpaper all over the air. And it creeps.
STEVE. Wish I could see it.
RACHEL. You probably could if you poisoned yourself like I did. I mean it probably is just what's there to see, like what you're seeing is what's there to see.
STEVE. Except then how come all the rest of the time we see what I'm seeing now? I mean, leaving aside the old one about whether we both do see the same thing the rest of the time.
RACHEL. Wait—I've got to go around again. Oh, there. I mean, I've just dumped some chemicals into my brain that don't accord with my ... my, you know, perceptual apparatus, or whatever. I mean I bet all species probably have these, like, different sensory coordinates or something, and you're just on one axis or another. I mean after all, why would a goldfish and an elephant even see the same colors, you know? Get the same part of the spectrum as each other? I mean each one probably sees this whole world that's invisible to the other one!
STEVE. Could be.
RACHEL. So, oh, you know what? Oh, no! I've got it! You know what's true?
STEVE. No. I don't. What's true.

RACHEL. What's true is that there's something that's real, but we don't know what it is. And we can't know what it is, and we'll never know what it is, cause all we've got is the thing we know things with, which can't know things it isn't equipped to know. All we can even imagine is stuff we *can* imagine! I bet we're just absolutely swimming in stuff we don't even know is there.

STEVE. Well, I don't see why you think anything's there at all.

RACHEL. Well, cause obviously there is. We just don't have any access to it.

STEVE. Well, but look, Rachel. Come on. I mean, why don't you think it works the other way around? Why wouldn't there be *nothing* out there? I mean, I know it seems like you and I are having this conversation and everything—at least, I suppose it must seem like that to at least one of us—but how can you be sure it's not just an experience in your own mind? Or even just an experience in some—uh—experiencing mechanism that you interpret as your own mind?

RACHEL. But that's just so, sort of, *old fashioned*. I mean it's so, so *anthropocentric*. I mean, that makes it seem like thought is so, uh, *central*. But, see, the whole point is, it isn't! It's just some sort of adaptive detail, like having a shell, is the thing! Hey, this is important—are you there?

STEVE. I think so.

RACHEL. See, this means—oh how depressing! How depressing! This means that thought is just this little physiological function of preservation. See? Bugs know how to make huge quantities of bugs to keep their species going, and we can figure out how to start a fire to keep ours going. All this other stuff, *thinking*, you know—Socrates... The New York Review... it doesn't mean a thing! None of it! Going bowling, for instance! Meaningless! Thinking doesn't necessarily go anywhere! It's not supposed to! It's just a by-product, an evolutionary leftover, get it? Bugs make bugs, and people think. Oh, God!

STEVE. Cheer up. It could be worse.

RACHEL. How! It couldn't be. How could it be worse?

STEVE. Could be us making those bugs.

RACHEL. Oh, yeah.

STEVE. And anyhow, Rachel. Besides. If there is something there, which I, for one, frankly doubt, what difference does it make whether we know what it is? The main thing is that it's there, right? I mean, if that really is what you think. So just, you know, cheer up. (*He pulls a blanket around himself and turns away to fall asleep.*)

RACHEL. (*To herself*) Well, I think it's depressing. (*She tries to read a comic, but can't make any sense of the print. She strolls up to* MELANIE's *false eyelashes for a little conversation.*) Hi, guys. I see you wiggling. You alive, there? Huh? Why not? Only God can make the things people make into things to make false eyelashes out of. Right? Oh, well. You guys rest.

DECEMBER
(24)

(RACHEL *is eating out of a box of Sugar Pops.* MELANIE *walks in with an enormous bag of groceries, and as they talk she brings in bag after bag.*)

RACHEL. Gee! Food?
MELANIE. Seems we're having a Christmas party here.
RACHEL. Us? How come?
MELANIE. Well, Edie and Sue invited a whole bunch of people to their place, but one of their pipes froze, and they don't have any water, so I said we could do it here.
RACHEL. Oh. When is Christmas, anyhow?
MELANIE. Tomorrow.
RACHEL. Oh. Weird. So who's coming?
MELANIE. Oh, Edie and Sue and Sanford, of course. And there's this great looking set of humanoids from Colorado who are crashing with them. And Sue's Keith. And Jeremy's coming, with some friends of his.
RACHEL. What about those religious people who're living at Edie and Sue's?
MELANIE. Oh, yeah. Mark and Louise. They're bringing their own grain. And Ruthie Fisher, and Robbie from the Wellspring, and Marty Patera, and

Hoffmeier and Annie, and Megan March, and Megan Fierstein, and all the people from The Horse's Mouth, and, oh, I don't know, about 2 million other people, I think. I can't remember exactly who.

RACHEL. Wow. Hey, where did you get the money for all this food?

MELANIE. Oh, I borrowed it.

RACHEL. From who?

MELANIE. Big Richie, actually.

RACHEL. Melanie.

MELANIE. Oh, it's all right. I mean, he's not exactly coming through with that job he promised me, so I don't feel bad about borrowing money from him.

RACHEL. But, uh, you know, I mean, do what you want, but he really is disgusting.

MELANIE. Well, true. But in some ways he's not so bad, really.

RACHEL. Like, uh, what ways?

MELANIE. Well, I don't know. Some ways. He has some good qualities.

RACHEL. Like what good qualities?

MELANIE. Well, just some good qualities, in general.

RACHEL. But, like, in particular, what good qualities?

MELANIE. Oh I don't know. All right. So he's a nauseating horse's ass. He's not so bad though, really.

RACHEL. What do you mean, he's not so bad! He's a nauseating horse's ass, Melanie.

MELANIE. Well, so what. Someone has to be one, why not him.

RACHEL. So why are you borrowing his money?
MELANIE. Whose money am I going to borrow? ...see, Rachel?
RACHEL. I'm sorry. (*Long silence*) So how're we going to cook all this stuff?
MELANIE. Well, Edie's coming over to help us. And Steve's coming, and believe it or not he's bringing Celia.
RACHEL. I thought Edie was still mad at us about those dresses we didn't make.
MELANIE. The...?Oh! Oh, I don't think so. Why would she be?

(*A huge Christmas tree starts to enter the room, top first*)

RACHEL. Eeep!
MELANIE. Oh! There's Steve.
RACHEL. Funny, for a moment it looked like a huge...
STEVE. (*From off*) Oop. I think I may have (*Thundering crash*)...miscalculated a bit. (*He edges around the tree,* CELIA *behind him*) We can put it.. hummm. Let's see. Where can we put it.... (*He drags it across the room and props it up in a corner, at the steepest angle at which it will fit.*) I picked this one for its majesty.
RACHEL. It's very majestic, Steve.
MELANIE. And I like that angle. Sort of testimony to its majesty.

(*Long silence*)

STEVE. You know, it looks a bit...

CELIA. We should decorate it, is what.
MELANIE. Damn. You're right. But we don't have any ornaments.
RACHEL. Oh, you know what! We could make chains! Like out of newspapers!
MELANIE. Newspapers! Holy shit, Rachel.
STEVE. Newspapers? Oh, yeah. I saw one once. White with black stripes. Very decorative.
CELIA. You mean none of you read the paper?
MELANIE. Well, dear, people don't necessarily keep their old newspapers around in case they misplace their Christmas tree ornaments.
CELIA. How do you know what's going on if you don't read the paper?
RACHEL. Well, I figure that basically you either know what's going on or you don't. And if you basically don't, reading the paper just isn't going to help.
MELANIE. Let's see. Oh, I know. I've got lots of great underwear. We can use that.
STEVE. Good. What else—What about some of these nice cigarette butts?
MELANIE. Oh, yeah. We can hang them on the branches with little loops of thread, and they'll sort of twinkle.
CELIA. I'll draw an angel for the top. Got some paper and pencils?
MELANIE. Well! We are really taking the bull by the horns today, are we not. Why don't you two work on the tree, and Rachel and I will start cooking.
RACHEL. I don't know how to cook.
MELANIE. Here. I'll get you some things. (*She exits and returns immediately with underwear, needles and thread, and paper and pencils*)
MELANIE. Time for the staff to swing into action.

(MELANIE *and* RACHEL *exit to kitchen*)

(*While* STEVE *and* CELIA *talk, she draws, and he hangs underwear on the tree.*)

STEVE. Are you sorry you didn't go home for Christmas?
CELIA. Oh, no. I really wanted to stay here and be with you.
STEVE. Will your folks be very sad without you there?
CELIA. No—no.
STEVE. It must be terrific, Christmas at your place, with all your brothers and sisters.
CELIA. Well, we all manage to get through it alive. And there are moments when it's sort of fun—How do you make wings? Oh, there, that's right.
STEVE. I always wanted to grow up in the country,
CELIA. Steve, it's not the country, it's the suburbs. The suburbs are horrible!
STEVE. Does your family sing carols on Christmas?
CELIA. Steve, listen. Is there something you . . . What would you . . . I mean, Steve, would you rather I went home?
STEVE. What do you mean!? What are you talking about!? I just want you to have a nice Christmas, is all. I don't want you to be . . . disappointed.
CELIA. I want to be here, Steve. (*long silence*) Gosh. There are coffee cups all over the floor—
STEVE. Oh, that's all right. Just leave them there.

(EDIE *enters*)

EDIE. Hey, hi.
STEVE. Hi, Edie.

CELIA. Hi, I'm Celia.

EDIE. Yeah? That's great. God, we were all beginning to think you were one of Steve's fantasies. Hey, terrific vulture!

CELIA. Well, that's my angel, actually.

EDIE. Well, angels, vultures—they all eat dead people. So. where are Rachel and Melanie?

CELIA. In the kitchen.

EDIE. Good. I really came to help them. This really is nice of Melanie. I've been so pissed off at her about that business with Jeremy.

STEVE. Really? How come?

EDIE. Well, shit, I mean in addition to ruining Jeremy's relationship with about 20 customers who ordered those dresses she never came across with, she wrecked yards of my fabric. And Jeremy blamed it all on me, sort of, for a whole long while.

STEVE. Well, she really did plan to make those dresses.

EDIE. I know she planned to. But, like, she planned to make them, but she didn't actually make them. There's a difference. I really don't know how she gets out of one day into another.

STEVE. Well, she does ok. She comes through in a pinch.

EDIE. Like with those dresses.

STEVE. Well, she's ok basically, really. You just sort of have to be loose about what you think ok is.

EDIE. Ok!? You think Melanie's OK!? She's a real demolitions expert, Steve. I mean, she walks into a bar, it's full of nice old geezers having a little nip, by the time she's been there 15 minutes people are bashing each other over the head with chairs, breaking bottles on the bar, brawling on the floor; perfectly nice men in suits ask her out for dinner, and they end up dumping her out of their cars onto the highway, or she shows up a week later in bandages; she goes for a little spin and five other drivers sail off a cliff—ok! Are you serious? They're going to come snatch her off the street any second. That is, if she's lucky.

STEVE. Well.

CELIA. Well, it must be tough if your parents die when you're three, and you're adopted by a transvestite who doesn't speak any English.

EDIE. What! Where did you hear that shit!

CELIA. Melanie told me.

EDIE. See, that's just what I mean! Total crap. She grew up in New Canaan, like everybody else. Oh, well.

CELIA. Well... (RACHEL *enters*) Oh, hi, Rachel. How's it going in there?

RACHEL. You wouldn't believe how much food is out there. There are a bunch of turkeys and a couple of hams and oh, God, this mountain of bread. And the vegetables! The kitchen looks like Vietnam. You need a machete to find the sink.

EDIE. Great.

RACHEL. Except it's all raw. I don't know what we're going to do. Melanie is taking a pretty classical approach, but I think we'd better throw it all into a vat and boil it.

EDIE. Well, maybe I'll go in and help. And here, I'll pick up some of these...Jesus! There's a dead mouse under this cup!

RACHEL. Oh, yeah, well. (*Silence*) That's our mouse

cupping system. (*Silence*) Gee. I wonder how my cookies are doing. The last time I looked, they were puffing up like little toads.
STEVE. Well, it's how they taste, mainly.
RACHEL. I've never really had toad.
CELIA. God. Can you believe it's Christmas already?
RACHEL. No, it's amazing. You know, I was really planning to go back to the city in September. I wonder why.
EDIE. (*With deep, deliberate malice*) To have a career?
RACHEL. I'm sorry about the mice, Edie.
EDIE. Oh, it's all right. I just wasn't expecting one.
CELIA. Gosh. It's just like a real family Christmas.
EDIE. Yeah, wow. Christmas at home. Hey, what was the worst thing your parents ever did to you on Christmas?
CELIA. The worst thing...the very worst thing... let's see...Well, once when I was really little I made this ashtray for my grandparents, and it was really repulsive I suppose, but I thought it was so pretty, and—
STEVE. I hate this game!

At this moment there is an eruption of clamor and activity. MELANIE *enters from the kitchen with a tray of food, and some guys from Colorado arrive introducing themselves boisterously and making themselves at home. While to all appearances the people in the room are throwing themselves into a party, they must actually be effect-*

ing as fast as humanly possible the set changes for the next scene. There should be much noise (but no audible words) rising into a crescendo at which CELIA's *angel is placed with great fanfare at the top of the tree.*

Blackout.

If no Guys from Colorado are available, recorded noises, or some other means must be used during the set change to create the impression of an extremely active party, after which there will be the dim stillness of:

DECEMBER
(26)

(*Sleeping bodies, one of which is* RACHEL's. STEVE *enters*)

RACHEL. Oh——! Hello?

STEVE. Oh, hi, Rache. It's me. Sorry to wake you up, but I left some hash here the other night, and Sue really needs something to calm her down. What are you doing out here?

RACHEL. It was cold in my room. Is Sue really upset about Melanie and Keith?

STEVE. Well, I think she's finally winding down to about homicidal.

RACHEL. I guess it was a bit tactless of Melanie. Specially since she knew Sue was coming back.

STEVE. Yeah, but, basically, who cares, really.

RACHEL. Particularly since it was bound to happen sometime or other. Probably everybody should be glad to have gotten it over with. Everything ok with Celia?

STEVE. Oh, yeah.

RACHEL. Where is she?

STEVE. At her sister's, I guess. Are these those guys from Colorado?

RACHEL. Yes! Aren't they beautiful?

STEVE. Well...

RACHEL. Look—see how snuggly they are? Look at those bright parkas! And see their hair? How rich and silky it is? Look—See? It's like some...some imported delicacy—See? Come feel it—And have you seen their boots?

STEVE. Oh, yeah. They're just like mine.

RACHEL. They are? Oh, yeah. Weird. Steve, remember a long time ago I said that I thought that when anybody said something it was the truth?

STEVE. No.

RACHEL. Well, you were about to tell me why you didn't agree, but we were interrupted. But why don't you agree?

STEVE. Well, let's see. If I really don't agree I suppose it's because you only know all of what someone is trying to tell you if what they say...corresponds to fact. But if what they say doesn't correspond to fact, you have to know what the facts are in order to know what it is that the person is trying to tell you. I mean, if Melanie says she was adopted, that's what she's telling you if she really was adopted. But if she wasn't, she's still telling you something, but you can't know what it is unless you already know she wasn't adopted.

RACHEL. Oh, I see. You mean that there's a difference between things that are true and things that aren't.

STEVE. I guess that is what I mean.

RACHEL. I should have known that, shouldn't I. (MELANIE *enters*) Oh, did we wake you up, Melanie?

MELANIE. No. One of the blonds is in there asleep and he's tossing and turning and moaning and groaning like my bed was hell or something.

STEVE. Why don't you wake him up and tell him to sleep out here?

MELANIE. I don't know. It just seems easier to sleep out here myself.

STEVE. Oh, Melanie—is there any of that hash left? I'd like to bring Sue some to console her.

MELANIE. Oh, sure. Here. And take it from me. She'll definitely be getting the best of the bargain.

STEVE. Thanks. Well, see you. (STEVE *exits*)

RACHEL. Melanie—what would you really like to be? If you could be anything?

MELANIE. President. Do you think Sue's really angry at me about Keith?

RACHEL. Oh, well, I guess maybe. She tends to get angry about stuff. But it doesn't last.

MELANIE. Gosh. I feel bad about it, Rachel. I really do. It's just I figured, you know, that if she cared about him she wouldn't have left him lying out on the sofa where anybody could just pick him up and walk off with him.

RACHEL. Well, seems like she's pretty hung up on him.
MELANIE. I wonder why. He's such a zero, let me tell you, with his little pipe and his little jacket and that Mr. Tenure chuckle. He's just such an ingratiating pile of shit zero. I really don't know what on earth she's doing with him. I just can't believe she actually cares about him.
RACHEL. Well, it's odd. But that's the sort of thing you can just never really figure out.

FEBRUARY

EDIE. So what are you going to do if the house gets sold?
RACHEL. Gee, I really don't know.
EDIE. It won't get sold. Who would want it? The roof leaks, the floor slants, the wallpaper sucks, the pond is stagnant, there are junkies in the beds, mice under the cups. It won't get sold. At least not for a while.
RACHEL. Ruthie Fisher is pretty upset, I guess.
EDIE. What did she say?
RACHEL. I'm not exactly sure. Melanie talked to her. But the idea was, she's responsible to her office, and her office is responsible to the clients, and we're a public disgrace, and everyone knows we're destroying the house, kind of thing.

EDIE. Well, obviously she was talking about Melanie, not you.

RACHEL. Well, I don't know. I actually am here, as it turns out. It's strange, you know. I thought I was leading my life, but it turns out I'm representing it, you know? Like to the public. So everybody, except me, of course, knows what's going on. And everybody approves or disapproves or something. So weird, that it turns out that what a person is, is a...an *issue*.

EDIE. Well, everybody around here does tend to know everything about everybody else. And Melanie's sort of worn out her welcome. Is she feeling better, by the way?

RACHEL. Oh, definitely. She's fine, essentially. She sleeps a lot, but her leg is all better, except for some marks.

EDIE. It's amazing she's alive. People don't generally slam into a tree at 60 and come out a little sleepy. She's too lucky for her own good. She'll never learn. Anyhow, tell her I came by to say hello.

RACHEL. Ok. She'll be glad you stopped in.

(EDIE *exits.* MELANIE *appears in the doorway of her room*)

MELANIE. Has shithead left?

RACHEL. Oh, you're up! How are you!

MELANIE. Fine. You know, much as every turd in this town would like me to be hideously mangled and totally incapacitated at the very least on the one hand, on the other hand they'd really resent having to feel sorry for me or having to take back any of the things they say about me.

RACHEL. Could that be true, do you think?
MELANIE. Oh, Rachel. Jesus.
RACHEL. You know—I keep feeling like something's up, what with you bashing into that tree, and the house getting sold, and Steve and Celia splitting up. Do you feel like something's up?
MELANIE. Well, maybe.
RACHEL. What is it, do you think?
MELANIE. The usual: nothing.
RACHEL. I guess so.
MELANIE. Want a drink?
RACHEL. I'm restless. I feel like doing something.
MELANIE. How about sitting around and getting loaded.
RACHEL. Sounds good. Hey, oh boy. It's Celia! Hi, Celia, come on in.
CELIA. Hi. I came to see how you were and, well, just to say hello. Or goodbye, really. I mean, I've really enjoyed knowing you two, even though we don't really know each other at all, and I just wanted to come say that, cause I don't suppose we'll really see each other any more.
RACHEL. Why not?
CELIA. Well, it looks like Steve and I aren't going to be seeing any more of each other, you know, so I probably won't see you two, either, even though I'd like to. But that's just the way things work out, isn't it? Even if nobody wants it to be that way.
MELANIE. Yup. That's certainly one thing you can say about men. When they dump you, you lose all your friends. Well, let's cement the end of our association with a little dope.

(*They light and pass a pipe.*)

RACHEL. Why are you and Steve breaking up anyhow? I don't really get it.

CELIA. Well, we're just not getting along too well these days, I guess. In fact, I'm not sure if we ever did.

RACHEL. Gee, it's hard to imagine you fighting.

CELIA. No. We didn't really fight.

RACHEL. Well, I mean, what happened? I thought you were crazy about each other.

MELANIE. Hey, Rache. You're getting a bit intense there.

CELIA. It's ok. I mean, I really, really like Steve, but when you get right down to it, he isn't actually interested in me. He thinks he is, but it's the idea he likes, really, or some picture he's got of me, but it's not me he cares about. It's awful, actually. He really believes he does care about me, but, you know, no matter how much I'd like to believe it, I can see that he really just doesn't.

STEVE. (*Appearing in the doorway*) Oh, sorry. I just stopped in to see if you needed help with the wood.

MELANIE. Oh, thanks. No, though.

STEVE. Well, I guess I'll just be off, then.

CELIA. Oh, it doesn't matter.

STEVE. No. I didn't mean to interrupt you.

CELIA. It doesn't matter. You might as well stick around.

STEVE. I'm really sorry. I didn't see your car.

CELIA. Look. I said it's all right. I don't mind.

Don't worry, I'm not going to fall apart. (*Silence*) I'm sorry.

STEVE. That's ok. How are you?

CELIA. I'm ok. How are you?

STEVE. Oh, ok. I'm ok.

MELANIE. Well, since we're all ok we might as well all sit down. Sit down, Steve. Drugs? Alcohol?

STEVE. Oh, drugs, thanks.

(*They continue to smoke*)

RACHEL. But, listen. What *is* going on.

CELIA. You mean, like... What do you mean? How?

RACHEL. Well, everyhow, I guess.

MELANIE. Nothing is going on, Rachel, except just the things that go on—We're sitting around smoking a little dope, and Steve and Celia are both here, which is a bit strange, maybe, and well, that's about it, really. And you feel like you don't know what's going on, and that's all, you know. Just stuff. Don't worry about it.

RACHEL. I'm not worried. I just have this feeling that I could sort of understand something. But I don't. Hey, Celia—Come talk to me. We've never really talked to each other and maybe we could. I mean, we might just be able to.

(RACHEL *takes* CELIA *into another part of the room, and the following conversations between* RACHEL *and* CELIA, *and between* STEVE *and* MELANIE *run concurrently.*)

RACHEL. I mean, why couldn't this be the time and place, you know? I mean, why couldn't this be the moment of all moments, when we could just sit right down and *understand* something. I mean, don't you ever feel like you just almost could? That you might just jump up on the table *right now* and say, "Oh, wow, this is preposterous! Clearly the real situation is blah-blah!" You know?

CELIA. Yes... I do know. I do feel like that sometimes.

RACHEL. Yes...?

STEVE. Oh, things are so bad.

Oh, God.

STEVE. I don't know why she can't believe how much I care about her. I've got to leave.

RACHEL. So why don't we? I mean, why spend your life not understanding anything! When you could just. Understand something!

CELIA. Yes . . . that's true...

RACHEL. So let's! Right now.

PASTORALE

CELIA. Ok.

RACHEL. So?
CELIA. Well, I'm trying. God. This is really hard!

CELIA. Rachel, do you smell something funny?
RACHEL. See! We just won't do it! We'll just distract ourselves in any way we can!
CELIA. It's true. That's true.
RACHEL. Let's really really concentrate.
CELIA. Ok. This time I'm really going to do it!

STEVE. I've got to settle down somewhere. Celia's going to be a doctor, did you know? Oh, I can't stand this.

STEVE. Anyhow, how are you?
MELANIE. Oh, just great, thanks, Steve. Never better. I mean, what do you think? I've just driven my car into a tree, it turns out I'm a well-known nutcase, I'm stone broke, and any minute I might not have a place to live!
STEVE. Melanie—

STEVE. Come on, Melanie —Cheer up!

CELIA. Is that smoke?

RACHEL. You're not trying!

CELIA. I know, but I think that's smoke somewhere!

RACHEL. Oh, we'll never do it!

CELIA. Rachel, I know what this seems like, but I think the sofa's on fire.

RACHEL. You see! We'd do anything to get out of this! We'd give anything to not just understand something!

CELIA. It's true. You're right! You're absolutely right! BUT WE NEED WATER!

MELANIE. Well, thanks, Steve, but I'd rather not, if you don't mind. Just this once, I'd really rather not. I'd rather figure out what to do.

STEVE. Aw, Melanie.

STEVE. Melanie, Jesus.

STEVE. Don't feel so bad, Melanie.

MELANIE. But I do feel bad! I feel horrible! But I don't care how I feel! See, the thing that's actually at hand, is what do I do now, Steve? What the hell am I GOING TO DO!?

(STEVE, MELANIE, RACHEL, *and* CELIA *stand frozen, facing the couple that has just entered. The sofa billows revolting black smoke.*)

MAN. Hello—We've come to look at the house. You know, your sofa's on fire. Maybe we should put it out before there's a problem.

APRIL

EDIE. So, you know, you could move into our place if you wanted.
RACHEL. Thanks. That's really great, but I think I'm going back to the city.
EDIE. The city? Really? It's so crazy there, though. How come?
RACHEL. Well, you know, I was really only planning to stay up here for the weekend.
EDIE. Well, good luck.
RACHEL. Thanks.
EDIE. Are you really upset about Melanie?
RACHEL. No. Why—you mean because she's going to live with Big Richie?
EDIE. Yeah.
RACHEL. No, why?
EDIE. Well, I thought you might feel guilty or something.
RACHEL. Me? How come?
EDIE. I don't know. You really shouldn't. I just

thought maybe you'd feel like you should have taken better care of her.

RACHEL. I think it's a good thing, actually.

EDIE. Huh? How could it be good? I mean, you know what? Melanie's got a lot of good qualities, actually, buried in that mess she's made of herself. Remember her at school? And if she's just looking for some guy to support her she could do better than Richie. I mean, if she would just get herself a bit together.

RACHEL. Well, the thing is, though, he's there. And he actually likes her.

EDIE. Well, that's great, but he's so repulsive.

RACHEL. Well, he actually likes her. And he respects her. And he's very nice to her. He'll take care of her. Why not, for a while? It's either that or she'll have to hire some truck to come run her over.

EDIE. Well... (MELANIE *appears in her doorway*) Hey, hi!

MELANIE. Hello. No, wait...how about...let's see —'Drop dead, you piece of shit.'

EDIE. Listen. I know you're going to feel really bad about saying that to me, but you really don't have to, cause I know you're really unhappy and screwed up. So I'm not going to be all hurt or anything. Bye, Rachel.

(*She exits*)

MELANIE. Feeling more cheerful?

RACHEL. Yes, thanks.

MELANIE. This is good, it really is. Everything's

working out fine. We'll miss each other, but you can come up and stay with us whenever you want. Richie's house is very big, you know, and he's going to get some horses.

RACHEL. Well, here's Steve finally.

(STEVE *enters*)

STEVE. Hi. Hi, house. Can you believe some people are going to be living here? Look at this house! It's so—it's so full of—of meaninglessness.
MELANIE. Yeah. I don't feel like being here, now, at all. We really don't belong here.
RACHEL. We've got hours before my bus leaves. Maybe we should go into town.
MELANIE. Town. I sure don't want to see any of those people.
STEVE. You know what? We could take a walk.
RACHEL. A walk?
MELANIE. God. Well, we could, though. It's sort of warm out, actually.
STEVE. Yeah. It's warm, and it's still light. We could walk up on the mountain.
MELANIE. You know, I've never been up there.
RACHEL. Me either.
STEVE. So let's, maybe.
MELANIE. Yeah, let's.
RACHEL. Ok, let's.
MELANIE. Ok, get your sweaters. Here.

They stand together and step forward slightly. The walls fade, becoming a moving background of bare trees, and perhaps there are sounds, at first hardly audible. Distant chiming, for instance, and faint animal calls.

RACHEL. Look!

STEVE. Yeah.

RACHEL. Oh, remember this? Remember when it's spring?

MELANIE. Yes, it's strange. I always forget. Every year I've forgotten all about it and then, suddenly, there it is one day, and I feel all the ways I've felt every year before.

STEVE. Yes. I remember when the ground feels like this, resilient, sort of, with things moving under the top layer.

RACHEL. And the air is just sort of a thin veil, like this, with the sun right there behind it, and you can feel it next to your skin.

MELANIE. I remember when I was really little, playing outside in the spring when the snow was just only in little patches, little late patches, melting. And I remember making dams out of strawey stuff, and the snow would melt in shiny ribbons around them, and I pictured the earth spinning slowly with me standing up on it and a web of little melting streams all around it, all dark and glassy on the other side, and bright on top, where I was standing in the sun.

RACHEL. Yes. The little pale sun.

STEVE. Yes. So pale, this time of year, things. So thin and bright. Like everything shows, you know? Like the snow has been peeled away, and nothing has grown up yet to hide anything—the leaves or the grass or heat in the air, or that thick light—instead it's all there, you know, just for a moment. It's almost transparent, but it's right there, and for a moment you can almost see exactly what sort of thing it is—what sort of thing it is.

(Sounds, spinning trees, dark.)

PROP PRE-SET LIST

Onstage
    Sofa w/quilt
    Table
    Chair
    Stool
    Coatrack w/June dressing
    Bowl on table shelf containing:
        Hash, 3 pill bottles, extra cigarettes, **extra** candle, & matches
    Dec. 26 candle in compartment behind sofa
    Cigarette case w/lighter on table
    Fireplace cover in position

Offstage
    Coatrack dressings
    Coffee tray w/milk & sugar
    4 coffee mugs
    Ceramic ashtray
    Towel
    Bourbon & glass
    Large bag full of popcorn
    Aspirin & glass
    Bowl w/apples
    7 mousecups
    Mouse
    Glass ashtray

Magazines
Tray w/gin, tonic, lemon, knife, 3 glasses
Box of Sugar Pops
Comic book
Cigarette butts
8 bags groceries
Christmas tree
Bundle of underwear, bag, pencil, & scissors
Tray w/crackers & dip
Edie's candle
Box of Animals crackers
Apron
2 cooking mitts
2 blankets
Plate w/snowballs (1 quartered on cardboard tray)
Trash
Pack of cigarettes
Matches
Sears catalogue
2 suitcases

COSTUMES

RACHEL
  June:
    Blue jellies
    Lavender striped T shirt
    Blue navajo belt
    Blue stretch jeans
  August:
    Rose knitted tank top
  Sept:
    Blue/white/brown plaid flannel shirt
    Brown socks
  Nov:
    Brown stockings
    Slate blue long sleeve leotard
    Brown rayon print skirt
    Denim jacket
    Navy blue zip front sweatshirt
  Dec:
    Red/grey/turquoise plaid woolen shirt
    Red knitted slipper-socks
    Aqua apron
  Feb:
    Denim jeans
    Grey boot-slippers
    Blue woolen sweater

April:
　Yellow wool sweater

EDIE
　Sept:
　　Blue knitted skirt
　　Cowboy boots
　　Red turtleneck
　　Blue cotton guatamalen top
　　Paisley challis wool scarf
　　Slate blue knitted tights
　　Peachy-tan tote bag
　Dec:
　　White knitted dress with border
　　Purple metallic scarf
　　Blue knitted tights
　　Fur coat
　　Fur hat
　　Suede gloves
　Feb:
　　Olive green mohair sweater
　　Maroon/blue plaid blouse
　　Grape knickers
　　Maroon silk tie
　　Grape socks
　　Short roll-top brown boots
　　Cotton-print belt
　April:
　　Indian print cotton crinkle skirt
　　White petticoat
　　Blue cotton high-necked blouse

Purple/green tweed sweater
Cowboy boots

MELANIE
  June:
    Red striped belt w/flower
    White eyelet dress
    Red striped belt w lower
  August:
    Flounced beige print skirt
    Turg. blue crinkle top
  Sept:
    Black flat shoes
    Black stockings
    Black belt
    Black knit camisole
    Plaid 2-piece skirt and shirt
  Nov:
    Black velvet trousers
    Rose-colored sweater
    (Alternate—blue jeans
  Dec 26:
    Beige silk flowered kimono
  Dec 24:
    Cowboy boots
    Blue jeans
    Red turtleneck dickey
    Navy/white/red snowflake sweater
    Pink down vest
    Earmuffs-red
  Feb:
    Sweatpants
    Sweatshirt grey striped

"Rag" socks
April:
　Blue & pink flowered dress
　Lavender cardigan sweater
　Sheer stockings
　Beige pumps

CELIA
　Dec:
　　Beige cordoroy trousers
　　Pale green cotton turtleneck
　　Orange knitted sweater
　　Brown tweed hat
　　Plaid scarf
　　Duck-wader boots
　Feb:
　　Olive green chinos
　　Brown tweed sweater
　　Blue/white striped oxford shirt
　　Beige down jacket
　　Gloves

STEVE
　June:
　　Yellow bowling shirt
　　Blue jeans
　　Sneakers
　　Sneakers
　　Belt
　　Socks
　Sept:
　　Red muscle T-shirt
　　Cut-off blue jeans

    Red dance briefs
Sept:
    Brown T-shirt
    Olive green/gold plaid shirt
Nov:
    Blue gabardine shirt
    Grey wool vest
    Work boots
Dec:
    Blue/rose/white plaid flannel shirt
    Navy blue crew neck sweater
    Red knitted hat
    Gloves
    Blue parka with tan lining
Feb:
    Blue/white/red flannel shirt
    Thermal undershirt
April:
    Dark green plaid flannel shirt
    Greyish-blue wool crew-neck sweater

JOHN
    Denim jacket
    Denim jeans
    Black T-shirt
    Navy/white wool shirt
    Belt
    Cowboy boots

LAMBCHOP
    Green polyester pants
    White belt

Medallions - 2

COLORADIANS
    Bright blue parka
    Bright orange parka
    Navy survival jacket
    Navy/tan wool scarf
    Navy hat
    Red/navy scarf
    2 prs. work boots
      one high cut
      one low cut
    1 pr. work boots

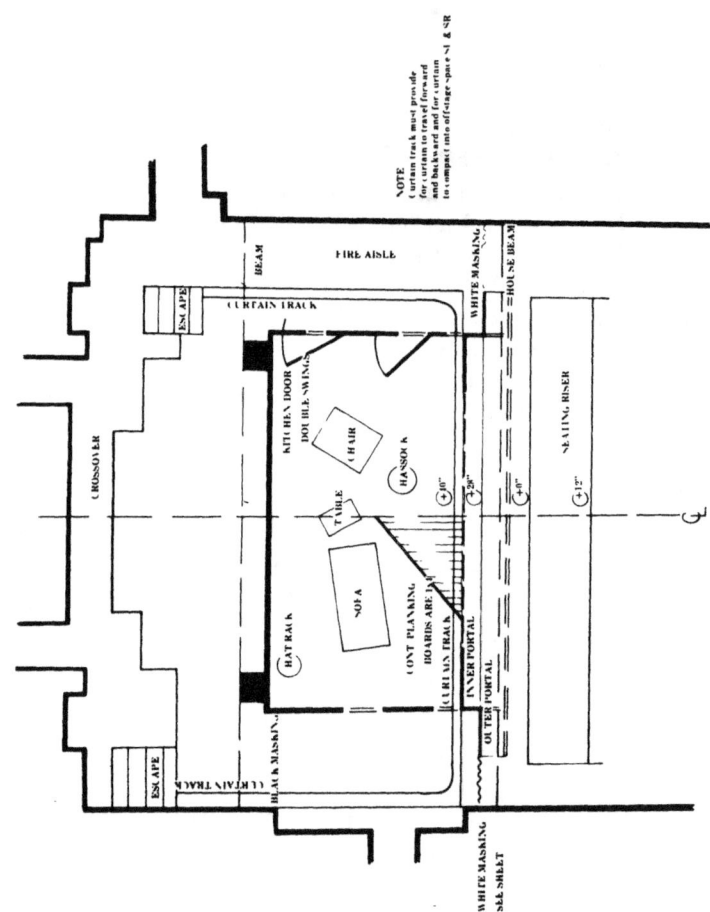

SKIN DEEP
Jon Lonoff

Comedy / 2m, 2f / Interior Unit Set

In *Skin Deep*, a large, lovable, lonely-heart, named Maureen Mulligan, gives romance one last shot on a blind-date with sweet awkward Joseph Spinelli; she's learned to pepper her speech with jokes to hide insecurities about her weight and appearance, while he's almost dangerously forthright, saying everything that comes to his mind. They both know they're perfect for each other, and in time they come to admit it.

They were set up on the date by Maureen's sister Sheila and her husband Squire, who are having problems of their own: Sheila undergoes a non-stop series of cosmetic surgeries to hang onto the attractive and much-desired Squire, who may or may not have long ago held designs on Maureen, who introduced him to Sheila. With Maureen particularly vulnerable to both hurting and being hurt, the time is ripe for all these unspoken issues to bubble to the surface.

"Warm-hearted comedy … the laughter was literally show-stopping. A winning play, with enough good-humored laughs and sentiment to keep you smiling from beginning to end."
- TalkinBroadway.com

"It's a little Paddy Chayefsky, a lot Neil Simon and a quick-witted, intelligent voyage into the not-so-tranquil seas of middle-aged love and dating. The dialogue is crackling and hilarious; the plot simple but well-turned; the characters endearing and quirky; and lurking beneath the merriment is so much heartache that you'll stand up and cheer when the unlikely couple makes it to the inevitable final clinch."
- NYTheatreWorld.Com

SAMUELFRENCH.COM

COCKEYED
William Missouri Downs

Comedy / 3m, 1f / Unit Set

Phil, an average nice guy, is madly in love with the beautiful Sophia. The only problem is that she's unaware of his existence. He tries to introduce himself but she looks right through him. When Phil discovers Sophia has a glass eye, he thinks that might be the problem, but soon realizes that she really can't see him. Perhaps he is caught in a philosophical hyperspace or dualistic reality or perhaps beautiful women are just unaware of nice guys. Armed only with a B.A. in philosophy, Phil sets out to prove his existence and win Sophia's heart. This fast moving farce is the winner of the HotCity Theatre's GreenHouse New Play Festival. The St. Louis Post-Dispatch called Cockeyed a clever romantic comedy, Talkin' Broadway called it "hilarious," while Playback Magazine said that it was "fresh and invigorating."

Winner!
of the HotCity Theatre GreenHouse New Play Festival

"Rocking with laughter...hilarious...polished and engaging work draws heavily on the age-old conventions of farce: improbable situations, exaggerated characters, amazing coincidences, absurd misunderstandings, people hiding in closets and barely missing each other as they run in and out of doors...full of comic momentum as Cockeyed hurtles toward its conclusion."
- Talkin' Broadway

SAMUELFRENCH.COM

TREASURE ISLAND
Ken Ludwig

All Groups / Adventure / 10m, 1f (doubling) / Areas
Based on the masterful adventure novel by Robert Louis Stevenson, *Treasure Island* is a stunning yarn of piracy on the tropical seas. It begins at an inn on the Devon coast of England in 1775 and quickly becomes an unforgettable tale of treachery and mayhem featuring a host of legendary swashbucklers including the dangerous Billy Bones (played unforgettably in the movies by Lionel Barrymore), the sinister two-timing Israel Hands, the brassy woman pirate Anne Bonney, and the hideous form of evil incarnate, Blind Pew. At the center of it all are Jim Hawkins, a 14-year-old boy who longs for adventure, and the infamous Long John Silver, who is a complex study of good and evil, perhaps the most famous hero-villain of all time. Silver is an unscrupulous buccaneer-rogue whose greedy quest for gold, coupled with his affection for Jim, cannot help but win the heart of every soul who has ever longed for romance, treasure and adventure.

THE OFFICE PLAYS
Two full length plays by Adam Bock

THE RECEPTIONIST
Comedy / 2m., 2f. Interior

At the start of a typical day in the Northeast Office, Beverly deals effortlessly with ringing phones and her colleague's romantic troubles. But the appearance of a charming rep from the Central Office disrupts the friendly routine. And as the true nature of the company's business becomes apparent, The Receptionist raises disquieting, provocative questions about the consequences of complicity with evil.

"...Mr. Bock's poisoned Post-it note of a play."
- *New York Times*

"Bock's intense initial focus on the routine goes to the heart of *The Receptionist's* pointed, painfully timely allegory... elliptical, provocative play..."
- *Time Out New York*

THE THUGS
Comedy / 2m, 6f / Interior

The Obie Award winning dark comedy about work, thunder and the mysterious things that are happening on the 9th floor of a big law firm. When a group of temps try to discover the secrets that lurk in the hidden crevices of their workplace, they realize they would rather believe in gossip and rumors than face dangerous realities.

"Bock starts you off giggling, but leaves you with a chill."
- *Time Out New York*

"... a delightfully paranoid little nightmare that is both more chillingly realistic and pointedly absurd than anything John Grisham ever dreamed up."
- *New York Times*

SAMUELFRENCH.COM

NO SEX PLEASE, WE'RE BRITISH
Anthony Marriott and Alistair Foot

Farce / 7 m., 3 f. / Int.

A young bride who lives above a bank with her husband who is the assistant manager, innocently sends a mail order off for some Scandinavian glassware. What comes is Scandinavian pornography. The plot revolves around what is to be done with the veritable floods of pornography, photographs, books, films and eventually girls that threaten to engulf this happy couple. The matter is considerably complicated by the man's mother, his boss, a visiting bank inspector, a police superintendent and a muddled friend who does everything wrong in his reluctant efforts to set everything right, all of which works up to a hilarious ending of closed or slamming doors. This farce ran in London over eight years and also delighted Broadway audiences.

"Titillating and topical."
- "NBC TV"

"A really funny Broadway show."
- "ABC TV"

SAMUELFRENCH.COM

www.ingramcontent.com/pod-product-compliance
Lightning Source LLC
Chambersburg PA
CBHW070649300426
44111CB00013B/2338